D1319919

The Richest Woman

IN BABYLON AND MANHATTAN

"Stylish Parables For Financial + Spiritual Health"

The Richest Woman
IN BABYLON AND MANHATTAN

With Seven *Timeless* Remedies
To Cure a Lean Purse

ANNETTE TERSIGNI R.N.

Cover Design by Annette Tersigni, Shane Willis, and Julie Csizmadia

Interior Layout and Design by Julie Csizmadia

ISBN-13: 978-1468103465

ISBN-10: 1468103466

Library of Congress Control Number: 2011944274

Printed in the United States of America

First Printing, 2012

Designed and Published by

CONSCIOUS BOOKS PRESS
Beaufort By the Sea, North Carolina
www.consciousbookspress.com

Dedicated to my father Joseph L. Tersigni who taught me everything he knew about money and to George S. Clason who taught me the rest.

To all my blessed spiritual teachers, my nursing and yoga colleagues, patients, students, friends worldwide and

To hardworking women everywhere, I bow to you.

CONTENTS

BABYLON

MANHATTAN

YO AND BEHOLD:

Financial & Spiritual Health is bountiful for those who know the *'seven timeless remedies'* for how to get it...keep it...and make it grow.

1. FATTEN your purse

2. CONTROL your expenditures

3. MULTIPLY your moolah

4. GUARD your treasure from loss

5. BUILD your home into a profitable investment

6. INSURE a future income

7. INCREASE your ability to learn and earn

ABOUT THIS BOOK

Many moons ago when I was a mere sprite of a girl, I read *"The Richest Man in Babylon"*. It changed my view about money for life. It is my sincere desire that this book, *"The Richest Woman in Babylon and Manhattan,"* will change 'your' life.

More recently, in these modern times of struggle for women, while driving home after teaching a stress management seminar at my local hospital, I was suddenly inspired with a vivid vision! It occurred while I was thinking about making one of my routine deposits into my savings account at the bank.

All the attendees at my seminar that day were women who were employees at the hospital. They included nurses, pharmacists, social workers, Internet techs, administrative assistants, educators, and upper and middle level managers. Hard working smart women who were all freaked out and fearful about their jobs, looming streamlining, (meaning job cuts) and the ailing economy. They were all sick, stressed, anxious and depressed about their money worries.

My spiritually based guidance helped to relieve their stress and inspire their souls, yet I couldn't help but wish that I could have offered them some financial guidance too. Then while driving to the bank, the vision hit me like a thunderbolt from the goddess of money. That thunderbolt resulted in my writing this book that you are holding in your hands, inspired by the late, great GEORGE SAMUEL CLASON.

Dear darling, brilliant, George was born in Louisiana, Missouri, on November 7, 1874. Beginning a long career in publishing, he founded the Clason Map

Company of Denver, Colorado, and published the first road atlas of the United States and Canada. In 1926, he issued the first of a famous series of pamphlets on thrift and financial success, using parables set in ancient Babylon to make each of his points. These were distributed in large quantities by banks and insurance companies and became familiar to millions, the most famous being "The Richest Man in Babylon", which is now part of public domain.

The Richest Woman in Babylon and Manhattan' is my adaptation of the original; comparable in the way that Hollywood filmmakers discover a great old classic then revise it for modern times. Mr. Clason's 'Babylonian parables' have become an inspirational classic. Of course, in those days, the leading characters in the book were all men. Times have changed.

My new version of this classic presents women in all the leading roles, starring in light hearted easy to read parables. I include the seven timeless remedies, which fattened my own once lean purse and enriched my formerly impoverished soul. *I give the essential blueprint on how to get money, keep money, and make money earn more money.* In addition, to further serve the reader, I have highlighted the importance of spiritual practices, which are not discussed in the 1926 version.

My life is now brimming with physical, financial and spiritual abundance. This abundance is available for you. It is never too late to learn and earn. You need only to take action and *apply the remedies.* It is my hope that my book, too, becomes an inspirational classic, bestowing riches in women's purses as well as in their souls.

May it bring you many Ah Ha's and ring bright notes of truth.

"The truth is always in fashion." Annette Tersigni R.N.

FOREWORD

To you fabulous ladies from all walks of life, know that our prosperity as women depends upon the personal financial and spiritual success of each one of us as individuals. Success means accomplishments resulting from our own womanly works and inherent talents and brilliance. A step by step foundation and easy, "I can do this" framework is the key to our triumph.

This book of seven remedies for lean purses is a guide to your understanding ancient and present day laws of money + spirituality that apply to modern women. That, truly, is its purpose: to offer hard workingwomen financial and spiritual freedom, security and peace. I offer you a vision based in ageless wisdom, which will help you to get money, keep money and build your surpluses into new money-honey.

In the pages that follow we are taken to modern day Manhattan, recognized as the financial capital of the USA, and then back to ancient Babylon, the cradle of civilization which nurtured the basic principles of finance now recognized and used the world over.

To new readers, this author extends her heartfelt desire that these parables may contain for them motivation + inspiration for growing bank accounts, greater financial successes and the solution for difficult financial and spiritual problems.

We offer you the legendary genie in a bottle from Babylon and Manhattan.

Babylon became the wealthiest city of the ancient world because its citizens were the richest people of their time. They appreciated the value of money. They practiced sound financial principles in acquiring money, keeping money and making their money earn more money. They provided for themselves what we all desire...incomes for the future. The future is now.

Money is governed today by the same laws, which controlled it when prosperous men thronged the streets of Babylon, six thousand years ago. Times have changed. This is a book about women, by a women and for women, Manhattan women, and women throughout the USA, Canada, Europe, England, Australia; women in fact everywhere in the world. After all *we women control the purse strings and are responsible for 83% of all buying power!* It is time we understand the laws, financial and spiritual, which govern abundance for all women and indeed for all men.

Manhattan is a metaphor. I intersperse real and imaginary people and places, liberally borrowing from Babylon with a tasty, humorous twist. Take this story into *your own* hometown dear reader and seeker of wealth and wisdom. Share it with your sisters, your mothers, your girl friends, and your daughters.

With love from Annette Tersigni and on behalf of the late George S. Clason

A BRIEF HISTORICAL SKETCH
OF BABYLON

By George S. Clason (Edited by the author)

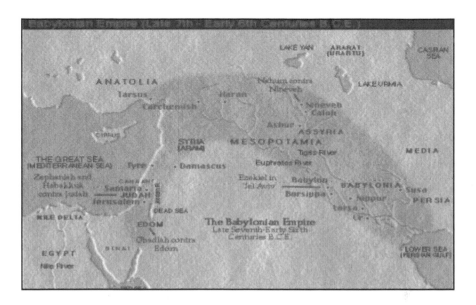

In the pages of history there lives no city more glamorous than Babylon. Its very name conjures visions of wealth and splendor. Its treasures of gold and jewels were fabulous.

Successive lines of kings to whom conquest and plunder were but incidental ruled Babylon. The outstanding rulers of Babylon live in history because of their wisdom, enterprise and justice. Babylon produced no strutting monarchs who sought to conquer the known world that all nations might pay homage to their egotism.

As a city, Babylon exists no more. When those energizing human forces that built and maintained the city for thousands of years were withdrawn, it soon became a deserted ruin. The site of the city is in Asia about six hundred miles east of the Suez Canal, just north of the Persian Gulf. The latitude is about thirty degrees above the Equator, practically the same as that of Yuma Arizona. It possessed a climate similar to that of this American city, hot and dry.

Today, this valley of the Euphrates, once a populous irrigated farming district, is again a wind-swept arid waste. Gone are the fertile fields, the mammoth cities and the long caravans of rich merchandise. Nomadic bands of Arabs, securing a scant living by tending small herds, are the only inhabitants. Such it has been since about the beginning of the Christian era.

Dotting this valley are earthen hills. For centuries, they were considered by travelers to be nothing else. The attention of archaeologists was finally attracted to them because of broken pieces of pottery and brick washed down by the occasional rainstorms. Expeditions, financed by European and American museums, were sent here to excavate and see what could be found.

Babylon was one of these. Over it for something like twenty centuries, the winds had scattered the desert dust. Built originally of brick, all exposed walls had disintegrated and gone back to earth once more. Such is Babylon, the wealthy city, today. A heap of dirt, so long abandoned that no living person even knew its name until it was discovered by carefully removing the refuse of centuries from the streets and the fallen wreckage of its noble temples and palaces.

THE RICHEST WOMAN IN BABYLON AND MANHATTAN

Many scientists consider the civilization of Babylon and other cities in this valley to be the oldest of which there is a definite record. Positive dates have been proved reaching back 8000 years.

In this way, we have proved that 8000 years ago, the Sumerites, who inhabited Babylonia, were living in walled cities. Their inhabitants were not mere barbarians living within protecting walls. They were an educated and enlightened people. So far as written history goes, they were the first engineers, the first astronomers, the first mathematicians, the first financiers and the first people to have a written language.

The glory of Babylon has faded but its wisdom has been preserved for us. For this we are indebted to their form of records. In that distant day, the use of paper had not been invented. Instead, they laboriously engraved their writing upon tablets of moist clay. When completed, these were baked and became hard tile. In size, they were about six by eight inches, and an inch in thickness.

These clay tablets, as they are commonly called, were used much as we use modern forms of writing. Upon them were engraved legends, poetry, history, transcriptions of royal decrees, the laws of the land, titles to property, promissory notes and even letters which were dispatched by messengers to distant cities. From these clay tablets we are permitted an insight into the intimate, personal affairs of the people.

Safely buried in the wrecked cities, archaeologists have recovered entire libraries of these tablets, hundreds of thousands of them.

One of the outstanding wonders of Babylon was the immense walls surrounding the city. The ancients ranked them with the great pyramid of

Egypt as belonging to the "seven wonders of the world." **Queen Semiramis** is credited with having erected the first walls during the early history of the city. From mention made by early writers, it is estimated they were about fifty to sixty feet high, faced on the outer side with burnt brick and further protected by a deep moat of water.

King Nabopolassar started the later and more famous walls about six hundred years before the time of Christ. Upon such a gigantic scale did he plan the rebuilding; he did not live to see the work finished. This was left to his son, Nebuchadnezzar, whose name is familiar in Biblical history.

The height and length of these later walls staggers belief. They are reported upon reliable authority to have been about one hundred and sixty feet high, the equivalent of the height of a modern fifteen-story office building. The total length is estimated as between nine and eleven miles. Of this tremendous structure, little now remains except portions of the foundations and the moat.

Against the walls of Babylon marched, in turn, the victorious armies of almost every conqueror of that age of wars of conquest. A host of kings laid siege to Babylon, but always in vain.

The city of Babylon was organized much like a modern city. There were streets and shops. Peddlers offered their wares through residential districts. Priests officiated in magnificent temples. Within the city was an inner enclosure for the royal palaces.

The Babylonians were skilled in the arts. These included sculpture, painting, weaving, gold working and the manufacture of metal weapons and agricultural implements. Their Jewelers created most artistic jewelry. Many samples have been recovered from the graves of its wealthy citizens and are now on exhibition in the leading museums of the world.

Babylonians were clever financiers and traders. So far as we know, they were **the original inventors of money as a means of exchange**, of promissory notes and written titles to property.

Hostile armies never entered Babylon until about 540 years before the birth of Christ. Even then the walls were not captured. The story of the fall of Babylon is most unusual. Cyrus, one of the great conquerors of that period, intended to attack the city and hoped to take its impregnable walls.

Advisors of Nabonidus, the King of Babylon, persuaded him to go forth to meet Cyrus and give him battle without waiting for the city to be besieged. In the succeeding defeat to the Babylonian army, it fled away from the city. Cyrus, thereupon, entered the open gates and took possession without resistance.

Thereafter the power and prestige of the city gradually waned until, in the course of a few hundred years, it was eventually abandoned, deserted, left for the winds and storms to level once again to that desert earth from which its grandeur had originally been built. Babylon had fallen, never to rise again, but to it civilization owes much.

The eons of time have crumbled to dust the proud walls of its temples, but the wisdom of Babylon endures.

Money is the medium by which earthly success is measured but it is not enough. Money makes possible the enjoyment of the best the earth affords if one is generous, kind and compassionate to others.

Money is plentiful for those who understand the simple laws, which govern its acquisition.

And now our modern day fable begins with:

The Woman Who Desired Gold

CHAPTER ONE

The Woman Who Desired Gold

Ambha, a rising star nurse entrepreneur and yoga teacher in Manhattan, was thoroughly discouraged. From her posh, designer silk yoga cushion, she sat and looked around bleakly at her humble 540 square foot crib on the Lower East Side. An elegant Mac computer displaying an unfinished Word doc rested at her feet.

So much for her meditation.

Her furtive glances on her manuscript reminded her that the refrigerator was almost empty and she should take action. It was time to realize her dream of writing a best selling book, hewing and polishing her antidote for the ailing health care system.

She was impassioned to 'expand consciousness in health care' hoping to get a book deal with a top New York literary agent and a *la dee da* publishing house that would deliver her regular fat checks to fill her *lean purse* and sagging bank account.

Nevertheless, her slender, not *so* saggy body sat stolidly upon her cushion, failing miserably at meditating. Her befuddled mind was struggling patiently with a problem for which she could find no answer to why she was stalled, making endless excuses to avoid getting her masterpiece completed.

The hot, muggy New York sun, so typical of this area in Manhattan, beat down upon her mercilessly. The air conditioning was on the fritz and beads of perspiration formed upon her brow and trickled down unnoticed to lose themselves in the cleavage of her ample bosom.

Nearby, cleaving the blue heavens was the painted tower of the Temple of Bellisima, New York, New York. In the shadow of such grandeur lay her simple abode and many others far less neat and well cared for. New York was like this—a mixture of grandeur and squalor, of dazzling wealth and direst poverty, crowded together without plan or system within the protecting confines of the Statue of Liberty.

Outside her window, had she cared to turn and look, the noisy cars beeped incessantly, crowded aside the stores and restaurants as well as the barefooted beggars. Even the walking rich were forced to turn into the pee stained gutters to clear the way for the long lines of homeless orphans of all ages, begging for alms as in the days of Babylon, the fabled richest city in the world.

Ambha was too engrossed in her own problem to hear or heed the confused hubbub of the busy, financial capital of America. It was the unexpected aromas of herbs and spices from the nearby kitchenette that aroused her from her reverie. She turned and looked into the sensitive, smiling face of her best friend—Melanie, a budding raw food chef, artist and caterer.

"May the Goddess bless you with great freedom forever and a day," began Melanie with an elaborate *namaste*. "It appears they have already been so generous you don't have to work. I celebrate your good fortune with a green smoothie, which I gladly share with you. Dear one, from your purse which must be bulging otherwise you would be busy writing, could you lend me two hundred lowly dollars until after the Buddha Groove Ball tonight? You won't even miss it until it's returned by the stroke of midnight."

"If I did have two hundred dollars," Ambha responded gloomily, "I couldn't lend it to anyone—not even to you, my best of friends; cuz that two hundred would be my fortune—my entire fortune. No one lends her entire fortune, not even to her best friend."

"What," exclaimed Melanie with genuine surprise, "You have bubkis in your purse and you sit like a statue on your cushion! Why not complete that manuscript! How else can you provide for your noble appetite? It's not like you my friend, where is your endless energy? Is something depressing you? Has the goddess brought you troubles?"

"A torment from the Goddess yes, that must be it," Ambha agreed. "It began with a dream, a senseless dream, in which I thought I was a woman of means. I was in Babylon, from my belt hung a silky purse, heavy with coins. There were shekels which I cast with careless freedom to the beggars; there were pieces of silver with which I bought a finery and teachers for my autistic son and whatever I desired for myself; there were pieces of gold which made me feel assured of the future and unafraid to spend the silver. A glorious feeling of contentment was within me! You wouldn't have known me as your hardworking friend. Nor would you have known my face, so free from the creases between my eyebrows, my worry lines, my face was shining with happiness. It was like back in the days when I was a top model, before I became a nurse and yoga teacher, and took a vow of poverty."

"Wow! What a dream," commented Melanie, "but why should such delish feelings that were aroused in you turn you into a glum statue on your cushion?"

"Why! Because when I woke up and remembered how empty my purse was, a feeling of rebellion swept over me. Let's talk it over together over our green smoothies, cuz as the sailors say, we're riding in the same boat. As young women, we went together to the church and the synagogue to learn wisdom. As grown women, we've gone to yoga diva teachers and their sanctuaries. We've always been close friends. We've been contented women entrepreneurs of our kind. We've been satisfied to work long hours and spend our earnings freely. We've earned a lot of coin in the years that have passed, but to know the joys that come from wealth, we have to dream about them. It totally sucks! Are we more than dumb, adorable, fashionable, spiritual and hip sheep? We live in one of the richest cities in the world. The tourists say nothing equals it in wealth and endless shopping possibilities.

"Manhattan has a huge display of riches, but we're settling for crumbs. After half a lifetime of hard labor, you, my best of friends, who has an empty bank account and empty knock off Louis Vuitton purse, say to me, "Can I borrow such a trifle as two hundred bucks until after the Buddha Groove Ball tonight?" Then, what do I reply? Do I say, "Here is my tacky purse; I'll happily share its contents with you darling? No, I admit that my purse is as empty as yours. What's up with that? Why can't we get the cash prize—more than enough for gourmet vegan food and a fabulous designer yoga wardrobe?

"Consider, also, your daughters and *all* the young women," Ambha continued, "aren't they following in the footsteps of their mothers? Do they as they go into the world and have their families, sons and daughters have to live their lives out of neediness, in the midst of such treasures everywhere, and yet, like us, be content to have a banquet of gluten free cereal with almond milk?"

"Never, in all the years of our friendship, have you talked like this before, Ambha." Melanie was puzzled.

"Never in all those years did I think like this before. From the wee hours of dawn until deep into the night and exhaustion stopped me, I have worked to expand consciousness with ancient yoga and modern nursing, building my website, my trainings, to really care for people with my sacred remedy and make a difference in the world, be a leader, a change agent, a medical activist, a health care rebel *with* a cause, soft- heartedly hoping some day the Goddess would recognize my worthy deeds and grant me great prosperity like in the ancient myths. She's never granted me that so called boon. At last, I realize she never will.

"My heart is wounded and sad. I want to be a woman of means. I want to own my own house, have a wellness center, study with great wisdom teachers, help my handicapped kid and his father in Montreal, and yeah, superficial as it sounds, I want to have a quality hemp, silk and linen, cool yoga wardrobe plus go on a few luxurious spa vacations and retreats, and some serious cash in my purse. Why do I feel like that's asking too much or maybe it's not my karma. I'm willing to work for these things with all the strength in my flexible spine, with all the skill in my hands, with all the cunning in my mind, but I want my efforts to be fairly rewarded. What is the matter with us?

"What the f@#k! Why can't we have our fair share of the fabulous, good things in life that are dripping off Manhattan women who have the big bucks to buy them?"

"Wish I had an answer!" Melanie replied. "I ask my self the same thing.

"My earnings from my catering bizz disappear in a flash. As a single mom, I have to plan and scheme so my girls don't go hungry, even if I am a chef. Also, in my heart of hearts, I have a deep longing to have my own show on the Food Network. I could really rock the meals that make love to my mind and turn on a whole new audience to the splendors of eating live, fresh, whole, mouth watering rainbow food, food glorious food. With my own show, I could make gourmet raw designer food finer than even the top chefs have tasted before."

"Dahlink, you should have such a show already. No woman in all Manhattan could do that show like you could; could make food taste of all the six tastes that the yogis teach in Ayurveda, that even the Hindu gods and goddesses would come to your table. But how the hell can we secure it while both of us are middle class working poor? Listen to the bell! Here they come."

She pointed out the window to the hoards of nine to fivers, long columns of exhausted women and men, rushing out of their symbolic sweat shops to the subways, modern slaves, marching together day after day, year after year with little happiness to look forward to.

"Pity the poor sheep. Melanie! Not so different from the slaves of Babylon who marched, bent under heavy goatskins of water doing the King's bidding."

"I do pity them and you make me see how little better off we are, free women though we call ourselves."

"That is the truth, Melanie, bummer of a thought though it be. We don't want to go on year after year living slavish lives. Working, working! Getting nowhere."

"Couldn't we find out how others make money and do it too?" Melanie inquired.

"Maybe there's some secret we might learn if we could meet up with the right people who know how to play the game," replied Ambha thoughtfully.

"Hmm. Earlier today," suggested Melanie, "I passed our old friend, Helen Gold, riding in her chauffeur driven Bentley. I have to say this; she didn't look over my humble head as many in her high falutin' station might consider their right. Instead, she waved her hand so all the gawkers could see her say hello and give her smile of friendship to Melanie, the raw food chef. Ha!"

"She *is* claimed to be the richest woman in all Manhattan," Ambha mused.

"So rich the President is said to seek her golden assistance in affairs of the treasury," Melanie replied. "So rich," Ambha interrupted, "I'm afraid if I met her in the dark, I might lay my hands on her fat designer purse."

"Nonsense," reproved Melanie, "a woman's wealth is not in the purse she carries. There's an old Babylonian saying that a fat purse quickly empties if there isn't a golden stream to refill it. Helen has an income that constantly keeps her purse full, no matter how liberally she spends."

"Income, that is the thing," shouted Ambha. "I wish an income that will keep flowing into my purse whether I sit on my cushion or travel to India. Or Italy. Helen *must* know how a woman can make an income for herself. Do you feel it's something she could make clear to a mind as muddled as mine?"

"I think she taught her knowledge to her twin daughters, Alisa and Jennifer." Melanie responded.

"Didn't she go to San Francisco and the word is she became, without help from her father, one of the richest women in that city *and* a patron of all things yoga?"

"Melanie, you're stimulating my mind." A new light gleamed in Ambha's eyes. "It doesn't cost anything to ask wise advice from a good friend and Helen was always that. And generous! Never mind that our purses are empty as the abandoned pigeon's nest on my balcony. We won't let that stop us. We're stressed out to the max from being without money in the midst of all this Manhattan uber abundance. We want to become women of means. Come on, let's go to Helen and ask how we can get some major moolah for ourselves."

"You're on fire, Ambha. You're bringing a new Ah Ha to my mind.

"You made me realize the reason why we've never found any measure of wealth. We *never* pursued it. You've worked your ass off patiently to build a new field in health care, in nursing and in yoga, and be an entrepreneur. You devoted your best to your mission and vision. And you've had awesome success. I struggled to become a skillful raw food chef and I've had success too.

"In the areas where we exerted our best efforts we both succeeded, girl friend. The Goddess was content to let us continue like this. Now, at last, we see the light. It's bidding us to learn more so we can earn more. With a new understanding we'll find honorable ways to accomplish our desires."

"Let's go to see Helen today," Ambha urged, "Also, let's ask our other girl friends who haven't done any better than we have, to join us so they can share in her wisdom."

"You were always mega thoughtful of your friends. That's why you have so many of them. It's going to play out as you say, my darling Ambha, yoga nurse. We'll go today and take them and all of our lean purses with us."

The Richest Woman In Manhattan

CHAPTER TWO

The Richest Woman In Manhattan

In old Manhattan there once lived a certain very rich woman named Helen Gold. Far and wide she was famed for her great wealth. Also she was famed for her kindness. She was generous in her charities. She was generous with her family and friends. She was liberal in her own expenses. But nevertheless each year her wealth increased more rapidly than she spent it.

And there were certain friends of younger days who came to her including Ambha and Melanie who had managed to strum up a crowd of Manhattan women who were carrying lean purses. Ambha, the nurse healer yogini, started the dialogue: "You, Helen, are more fortunate than us. You have become the richest woman in all Manhattan while we struggle to get by. You can wear the finest clothes and you can enjoy the best foods, while we have to be content if we can dress our families in clothing that is decent and feed and provide for them as best we can.

"Once we were equal. We studied under the same yoga masters. As girls, we played in the same games. And you didn't outshine us in the studies or the games. And in the years since, you've been no more honorable than us.

"Nor have you worked harder or more faithfully, so far as we can judge. Why, then, should a fickle fate single you out to enjoy all the good things of life and ignore us when we are equally deserving?"

Then Helen remonstrated, she had an effected way of speaking, partly hip modern and partly as if she came from a distant time, "If you haven't acquired more than a bare existence in the years since we were young, it's because you either have failed to learn the laws that govern the building of wealth, or else you don't observe them.

"Fickle Fate' is a vicious goddess who brings no permanent good to anyone. On the contrary, she brings ruin to almost every woman and man upon whom she showers unearned gold. She makes wanton spenders, who soon dissipate all they receive and are left beset by overwhelming appetites and desires they haven't the ability to gratify. Yet others whom she favors become misers and hoard their wealth, fearing to spend what they have, knowing they do not possess the ability to replace it. They further are beset by fear of robbers and doom themselves to lives of emptiness and secret misery.

"There are others probably, who can take unearned money and add to it and continue to be happy and contented citizens. But they're few, I know about them only by hearsay. Think of the women and men who have inherited sudden wealth, and see if these things aren't true."

Her friends admitted that of the women and men they knew who had inherited wealth these words were true, and they besought her to explain to them how she had come to posses so much prosperity, so she continued: "In my youth I looked about me and saw all the good things there were to bring happiness and contentment. And I realized that wealth increased the potency of all these. Wealth is a power. With wealth many things are possible.

"You can design your home with the richest of furnishings. You can travel the world. You can feast on the delicacies of the finest cuisine. You can be a philanthropist.

"You can buy dazzling, real gems from the top jewelers. You can donate to your spiritual teachers and even build enormous yoga temples for the Goddess.

"You can do all these things and many others in which there is delight for your womanly senses and gratification for the soul.

"And, when I realized all this, I decided to myself that I would claim my share of the good things of life. I wouldn't be one of those who stand on the sidelines, enviously watching others enjoy. I refused to be content to wear the cheapest clothing that looked fashionable. I wouldn't be satisfied with the fate of a poor woman. On the contrary, I would make myself a guest at this banquet of beauty and bounty.

"Being, as you know, the daughter of a humble shop keeper and owner of a deli on the Lower East Side, where some of you live today, I was one of a large family of sisters, with no hope of a decent inheritance, and not being gifted, as you've said so frankly, Ambha, with superior powers or wisdom, I decided that if I was to achieve what I desired, time and study would be essential.

"As for time, all women have it in abundance. You, each of you, have let time slip by, sufficient time to make yourselves wealthy. Yet, you admit my dear ones, you have nothing to show except your good name, your integrity and your families, of which you can be honestly proud.

"As for studying, didn't our wise yoga teachers and spiritual masters teach us that learning was of two kinds: the one kind being the things we learned and knew, and the other being the training that taught us how to find out what we didn't know?

"So I decided to find out how I might accumulate wealth, and when I had found out, I chose to make this my mission and do it with excellence. I mean, isn't it wise that we should experience life to the full while we live in the illumination of Mother Nature, the sorrows of the worldly life inevitably come to us, and our yoga teachings help our spirits to leave the body in peace when it is our time. Hmm?

"I found a job as an administrative assistant, used to be called a secretary, in a real estate firm working long hours each day. I juggled tons of tasks, typing up endless paper work before there were computers. Week after week, and month after month, I worked, but at the end of the week, I had borsht on my table and an empty purse. Food and clothing, travel to exotic places and donations to the temple, and other things I can't remember, absorbed all my earnings. But my determination never left me.

"And one day Tesh, the CEO big shot I dealt with from time to time, who was at the top of the ladder of a national bank, came to the real estate office. He had an affected way of talking as if he came from a distant place and time. Tesh ordered a copy of a Law regarding foreclosures on a project we were handling for him.

"I must have this in two days, and if the task is done by that time, I will give you a two hundred dollar bonus," he said.

"So I got on it working overtime, but the law was long and went on forever, so I took some time to party hearty, Ha! And when Tesh returned the tedious task wasn't finished.

"He was angry, and I lost the $200 bonus, if I had been his slave like in the days of Babylon, he would have beaten me. But knowing the owner of the real estate firm wouldn't allow him to get heavy with me, I wasn't afraid.

"Tesh, you are a very rich man. Tell me how I can become rich too, and I'll type all night and when the sun comes up, it *will be* completed." I said.

"Helen," he replied, "you're a forward little minx, but we'll call it a bargain."

"All through the night I typed although my typing skills were pathetic, while my back was killing me and the smell of the ribbon ink made my head ache until my eyes could hardly see. Still, when he returned first thing in the morning, the documents were done.

"Now," I whispered with baited breath, "tell me what you promised."

"You have fulfilled your part of our bargain, young lady," he said to me kindly, 'and I'm ready to fulfill mine. I will tell you these things you wish to know because I'm becoming an old man, and an old tongue loves to wag. And when youth comes to age for advice she receives the wisdom of years. But too often youth thinks that age only knows the wisdom of days that are gone, and therefore they don't learn or profit. But remember this, the sun that shines today is the sun that shone when your father was born, and will still be shining when your last grandchild will pass into the darkness.

"The thoughts of youth," he continued, 'are bright lights that shine like the meteors that make the brilliant sky, but the wisdom of age is like the fixed stars that shine so unchanged that a sailor can depend upon them to steer his course.

"Mark my words well, for if you don't you'll fail to grasp the truth that I will tell you, and you will think your night's work has been in vain."

"Then he looked at me shrewdly from under his shaggy brows and said in a low, forceful tone, "I found the road to wealth when I decided that a part of all I earned was mine to keep. And so will you."

"Then he continued to look at me with a glance that I could feel pierce me but said no more."

"Is that all?' I asked.

"That was sufficient to change the heart of a farmer into the heart of a prominent banker," he answered.

"But all I earn already *is* mine to keep, isn't?" I demanded.

"Far from it,' he replied. 'Don't you pay for your clothes at the trendy retailers, boutiques and department stores? Don't you pay the shoe store for your shoes? Don't you pay for the things you eat? Can you live in Manhattan without spending? What have you to show for your earnings of the past month? What about for the past year? Foolish girl! You pay everyone but yourself. Miss Helen Gold! Why don't you live to your name? You work for others. Go on and be a slave and work for what your master gives you to eat and wear. If you *did* keep for yourself one-tenth of all you earn, how much would you have in ten years?"

My knowledge of numbers did not let me down, it was the main reason I got the real estate job, and I answered, "As much as I earn in one year."

"You speak only half the truth Helen," he retorted. "Every dollar you save is a slave to work for *you*. Every penny it earns is its child that also can earn for you. If you want to become wealthy, then what you save must *earn*, and its children must earn, that all can help to give you the abundance and freedom you crave.

"You think I'm cheating you for your long night's work,' he continued, 'but I am paying you a thousand times over if you have the intelligence to grasp the truth I offer you.

"A part of all you earn is yours to keep. It should be not less than a tenth meaning ten percent, no matter how little you earn. It can be as much more as you can afford. *Pay yourself first*. Don't buy from the retailers more than you can pay out of the rest and still have enough for food and charity and donations to your place of worship and your spiritual guides.

"Wealth, like a tree, grows from a tiny seed. The first dollar you save is the seed from which your tree of wealth shall grow. The sooner you plant that seed the sooner the tree will grow. And the more faithfully you nourish and water that tree with consistent savings, the sooner you can bask in contentment beneath its shade." After saying this, he took his documents and went away.

"I thought a lot about what he had said to me, and it seemed reasonable. So I decided that I would try it. Each time I was paid I took ten percent from each paycheck and hid it in my kitchen cupboard. And strange as it may seem, I was no shorter of funds, than before. I noticed little difference as I managed to get along without it. But often I was tempted, as my hoard began to grow, to spend it for some of the cool things the shops were showing, I was young and wanted absolutely *everything* displayed at Macy's and Bloomingdales, and all the bohemian chic styles in SoHo. But I wisely refrained.

"A year after Tesh had gone he came back again and said to me, "Helen, have you paid to yourself not less than one-tenth of all you have earned for the past year?"

"I answered proudly, 'Yes, dear teacher, I have.' "That is good,' he answered beaming upon me, 'and what have you done with it?'

"I have given it to Marcus, a bricklayer, who told me he was traveling over seas and in Tunisia, he would buy me the rare jewels of the island of Djerba. When he comes home, we'll sell them at high prices and divide the earnings."

"Every fool must learn," he growled, 'but why trust the knowledge of a bricklayer about jewels? Would you go to the bread maker, the baker, to inquire about the stars? No, for heavens sake, you would go to the astrologer, if you had power to think. Your savings are gone, woman, you have jerked your wealth-tree up by the roots. But plant another. Try again. And next time if you want advice about jewels, go to the jeweler. If you want to know the truth about art, go to an expert art dealer. Advice is one thing that is freely given away, but watch that you take only what is worth having. She who takes advice about her savings from one who is inexperienced in such matters, will pay with her savings for proving the falsity of their opinions." Saying this, he went away.

"And it turned out exactly as he said. The Tunisians were crooks and sold my sexy brick laying Marcus worthless bits of glass that looked like gems. But I did what Tesh told me, I again saved ten percent of each paycheck, because by now, I had formed the habit and it wasn't hard anymore.

"Again, a year later, Tesh came to the real estate office and addressed me.

"What progress have you made since last I saw you?"

"I've paid myself faithfully,' I replied, 'and I've entrusted my savings to Antonio the jewelry designer, to buy silver to make his exquisite designs that sell well in all the high end shops, and every fourth month he pays me a percentage of his profits. This is what we commonly call "interest."

"That is good. And what do you do with the profits?' "I went to Bali on an exotic holiday and I've been able to eat at the Ritz for yummy lunches and sometimes even their high tea. Oh and I bought my first expensive face creams and had my first facial at Elizabeth Arden's Spa. And some day I'm going to buy a Volkswagen Beetle to drive to the Hamptons on weekends." To which Tesh laughed, "You're eating the children of your savings. Then how do you expect them to work for you?

"And how can they have children that will also work for you?

"First get a bankroll of dollars to be your slaves and then I hope you enjoy many a holiday and rich banquet without regret." And then he went away again.

"I didn't see him for two years, when he returned and his face was full of deep lines and his eyes drooped, I could see that he was becoming a very old man. And he said to me, "Helen, have you achieved the wealth you dreamed of?"

And I answered; "Not yet, I haven't achieved all that I want, but some I have and it earns more, and its earnings earn more. I'm now a top real estate agent for the firm. I am even thinking of starting my own business."

"And do you still take the advice of brick layers?" "About brick laying they give good advice," I laughed.

"Helen," he continued, "you have learned your lessons well. You first learned to live upon less than you could earn. Next you learned to seek advice from those who were competent through their own experiences to give it. And, lastly, you have learned to make money work for you.

"You have taught yourself how to acquire money, how to keep it, and how to use it. Therefore, you are competent for a responsible position. I am becoming an old man. My sons think only of spending and give no thought to earning. I have no daughter. My interests are great and I fear too much for me to look after. If you will go to San Francisco and look after my lands there, I'll make you my partner and you'll share in my estate."

"So I went to San Francisco and took charge of his holdings, which were huge. And because I was full of ambition and because I had mastered the three laws of successfully handling wealth, I was able to increase greatly the value of his properties.

"I prospered beyond my wildest dreams, and when the spirit of Tesh departed for the sphere of darkness, I did share in his estate as he had arranged under the law." Helen spoke, and when she had finished her tale, one of her friends said, "You were incredibly lucky that Tesh made you an heir."

"Lucky only in that I had the desire to prosper before I first met him. For four years didn't I prove my determination toward my purpose by keeping one-tenth of all I earned? Would you call a fisherman lucky who studied the habits of fish for years so that with each changing wind he could cast his nets around them?"

> **Opportunity is a haughty goddess who doesn't waste anytime with women who are unprepared.**

"You had strong will power to keep on after you lost your first year's savings. You're unusual in that way," spoke up another.

"Will power!" retorted Helen. "Nonsense. Do you think will power gives a single mother the strength to carry her burdens alone? Will power is but the unflinching *determination, purpose, single-mindedness, tenacity, drive, resolution, and perseverance* to carry a task you set for yourself to *fulfillment, success, self-actualization, self-realization, contentment, happiness and nirvana.* Let us pause, breathe deeply and meditate on this.

"You who seek also the riches for your spirits have heard of the word discipline but you do not *know* it. Hmm? Yet to be a disciple of wealth, be it worldly or spiritual takes discipline. To be a true disciple of wealth and wisdom you must discipline your small self to free your true Self with a capital S in all five of your senses.

"Be sensible ladies as well as sensual. If I set for myself a task, no matter how trivial, I see it through. How else can I have confidence in myself to do important things that can make a difference in this world? If I say to myself, 'For a hundred days as I walk across Central Park I'll repeat my sacred mantra,' I *do* it!

"If on the seventh day I took my walk without remembering, I wouldn't say to myself, tomorrow I'll say my mantra and that will be OK.' Instead, I would retrace my steps and repeat my mantra. And even on the twentieth day would I say to myself, 'Helen, this is useless. How does it benefit you to say your mantra everyday?' No, I wouldn't say that. When I set a task for myself, I complete it. Meditating every day is a boon in and of itself. It sets the way for discipline in other matters and opens the doors to riches like clarity and serenity in all things.

"So, I'm careful not to start difficult and impractical tasks, because I love leisure."

And then another friend spoke up and said, "If what you say is true, and it does seem what you have said is reasonable, then being so simple, if all women did it, there would not be enough wealth to go around."

"Wealth whether spiritual or worldly grows wherever women exert energy," Helen replied. "Your problem is you have poverty consciousness. If all women would meditate, wouldn't there be infinite spiritual wealth to go around? Is there a limit on consciousness, which is simply energy and information? Likewise money is a form of energy and spending it is energy exchange, a basic Newtonian law of physics that applies to your purse and your soul."

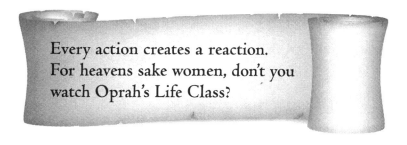

Every action creates a reaction.
For heavens sake women, don't you
watch Oprah's Life Class?

"If a rich woman builds herself a new mansion, is the money she pays out gone? No, the contractor and bricklayers have part of it and all the laborers have part of it, and the interior designer has part of it. And everyone who works on the house has part of it, yet when the palace is completed, isn't it worth all it cost? And is the ground, the land on which it stands not worth more because it is there? And is the land that adjoins it not worth more because it is there? Wealth grows in magic ways. No women can prophesize the limit of it. Didn't the ancient Babylonians build their great city on barren deserts with the wealth that came from their ships of commerce on the seas?"

"What then do you advise us to do so we can become rich too?" asked Melanie, the artistic chef and caterer. "The years have passed and we're no longer young women and we have nothing saved and many of us meditate which is the main reason we have endured for so long, still we long to have an easier life."

"I advise that you take the wisdom of Tesh and say to yourself,

"'A part of all I earn is mine to keep." Say it in the morning when you wake up. Say it at noon. Say it at night. Say it each hour of every day. Say it to yourself until the words stand out like burning letters engraved in the software of your soul.

"Impress yourself with the idea. Fill yourself with the thought. Then take whatever portion seems wise. It must not be less than one-tenth and put it away. Arrange your other expenditures to do this if necessary. But put away that portion, ten percent first. Soon you will realize what a rich feeling it is to own a treasure upon which you alone have claim. As it grows it will stimulate you. A new joy of life and security will thrill you.

"Greater efforts will come to you to earn more. As your earnings increase, won't the same percentage also be yours to keep?"

Then learn to make your treasure work for you. Make it your slave. Make its children and its children's children work for you.

"Insure an income for your future. Look at the aged and remember that in the days to come you too will be numbered among them. Therefore invest your treasure with the greatest caution that it is not lost. Exorbitant rates of return from many unscrupulous moneylenders in your communities and on the world wide Internet are deceitful sirens that sing but lure the unwary upon the rocks of loss and remorse.

"Provide also that your family is taken care of in case the Goddess calls you to her realms. For such protection it's always possible to make provision with small payments at regular intervals. Therefore the well-prepared woman doesn't delay in expectation of a large sum becoming available for such a wise purpose."

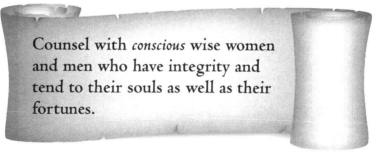

Counsel with *conscious* wise women and men who have integrity and tend to their souls as well as their fortunes.

"Seek the advice of those whose daily work is handling money. Let them save you from such an error like I made in entrusting my money to the judgment of Marcus, the bricklayer. A small return and a safe one are far more desirable than risk.

"Enjoy life while you are here. Don't overstrain or try to save too much. If one-tenth of all you earn is as much as you can comfortably keep, be content to keep this share. Live otherwise according to your income and don't become a cheapskate and afraid to spend. Life is good and life is rich with things worthwhile and things to enjoy."

Her friends thanked her and went away. Some were silent because they had no imagination and could not understand. Some were sarcastic because they thought that one so rich should divide with old friends not so fortunate. But some had in their eyes a new light. They realized that Tesh had come back each time to the real estate office because he was watching a woman work her way out of darkness into light. When that woman had found the light, a place awaited her. No one could fill that place until she had for herself worked out her own understanding, until she was ready for opportunity, to live her passion and calling in the world.

These latter were the ones, who, in the following years, frequently revisited Helen, who received them gladly. She counseled with them and gave them generously of her wisdom, as women of broad experience are always glad to do. And she assisted them in investing their savings so it would bring in a good interest rate with safety and would neither be lost nor entangled in investments that paid no dividends.

She introduced them to her friend Suze Orman and other women financial and spiritual gurus, entrepreneurs, visionaries and change agents who were making a difference in the world *and* making money.

The turning point in these women's lives came upon that day when they realized the truth that had come from Tesh to Helen and from Helen to them. *And the truth would make them free.*

PAY YOURSELF FIRST

Seven Remedies For a Lean Purse

CHAPTER THREE

The First Remedy—Start to Fatten Your Purse

Helen addressed an attentive woman in the second row. "My dear girl, what are you doing for a living?"

"I," replied the woman, "am an administrative assistant at an advertising agency."

"I started earning my first dollars as an administrative assistant too! That being said, you have the same opportunity to build a fortune."

She spoke to a deeply sun tanned woman, farther back. "Tell me, also, what do you do to pay your way?"

"I," responded this woman, "I'm an internet marketer. I design websites for women who want to be entrepreneurs and create their own online business."

"Because you also work and earn money, you have every advantage that I have to succeed."

In this way Helen proceeded to find out how each woman worked to earn her living. When she was done questioning them, she said:

"Now, my students, you can see that there are many professions and efforts at which women may earn money. Each of the ways of earning is a stream of gold you could say, from which the worker diverts from her labor a portion to her own purse. So into each of your purses flows a stream of coins large or small according to her ability. Right?"

Immediately they agreed that it was true. "Then," continued Helen, "if each of you yearns to build for your self a fortune, isn't it wise to start by employing that source of wealth which you've already established?"

They all agreed to this.

Then Helen turned to a humble woman who had declared herself an organic egg seller. "If you select one of your baskets and put ten eggs into it each morning and take out nine eggs from it every night, what will eventually happen?"

"In time my basket will be overflowing."

"Why?"

"Because each day I put in one more egg than I take out."

Helen turned to the class with a smile. "Does any woman here have a lean purse?"

First they looked amused. Then they laughed. Lastly they waved their purses of all shapes and sizes in the air jokingly.

"All right," she continued, "Now I'll tell you the first remedy I learned to cure a lean purse.

"Do exactly as I have suggested to the egg lady. For every ten dollars you put in your purse, spend only nine. Your purse will start to fatten immediately and its increasing weight will feel good in your hands and bring you satisfaction."

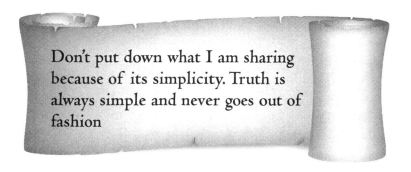

Don't put down what I am sharing because of its simplicity. Truth is always simple and never goes out of fashion

"I told you, I would tell you how I built my fortune. This was my beginning. I carried a lean purse too and cursed it because there was nothing inside to satisfy my desires. But when I began to take out nine out of every ten dollars that I put in to it, it began to fatten. So will yours.

"Now I'll tell you an inexplicable truth, and I really don't know the reason for it. When I stopped paying out more than nine-tenths or ninety percent of my earnings, and saved ten percent for myself, I managed to get along just as well. I was not shorter than before. Also, interestingly, more money came to me more easily than before. I feel it's a spiritual law of the Goddess; women who keep a certain part of their earnings and still manage to tithe to the needy in various charities, it seems money comes more easily.

"Likewise, it seems for a woman who has an empty purse, the goddess of abundance avoids.

"What do you desire the most? Is it the gratification of your endless desires each day for facials, jewelry, chukkas, better clothing, fine dining at trendy restaurants; things quickly gone and forgotten? Or is it substantial holdings, money, land, a profitable job, business or career, useful products and services, income-bringing investments? The money you take from your purse brings the first. The money you leave in it will bring the latter.

"This, my students, was the first remedy I discovered for my lean purse: 'For each ten dollars I put in, I spent only nine.' Debate this among yourselves. If any woman here proves it to be untrue, tell me tomorrow when we'll meet again."

The Second Remedy—Control Your Expenditures

CHAPTER FOUR

The Second Remedy—Control Your Expenditures

"Some of you, my dear students, have asked me this: How can a woman keep ten percent of all she earns in her purse when all the dollars she earns aren't enough for her necessary expenses?" This is how Helen addressed her students on the second day.

"Yesterday how many of you carried lean purses?" "All of us," answered the class.

"Still, you don't all earn the same amount of money. Some earn much more than others. Some have much larger families to support. Yet, all of your purses were equally lean. Now I will tell you an unusual truth about women. Whatever each of us calls our necessary expenses will always grow to equal our incomes unless we choose to differ and protest to the contrary.

"Don't confuse the necessary expenses with your endless desires. Each of you, together with your good families have more desires than your earnings can gratify. Your earnings are spent to gratify these desires as far as they will go and you still end up with a list of ungratified desires."

> **All women are burdened with more desires than they can gratify.**

"Because of my wealth do you think I can gratify every desire? Not true! There are limits to my time. There are limits to my strength. There are limits to the distance I can travel. There are limits to what I can eat. There are limits my passion and enjoyment.

"I'm telling you that just as weeds grow in a field wherever the farmer leaves space for their roots, so do desires grow freely in women whenever there is a possibility of their being gratified. Your desires are infinite and the ones you can gratify are few.

"Study thoughtfully your usual living habits. This is where most often you will find certain accepted expenses that can wisely be reduced or eliminated."

> **Let your motto be to demand one hundred percent satisfaction and value for each dollar spent.**

"So then, write down in a journal everything you desire to spend money on. Select those that are necessary and others that are possible through the expenditure of nine- tenths, or ninety percent of your income. Cross out the rest and consider them but a part of that great multitude of desires which must go unsatisfied and don't regret them."

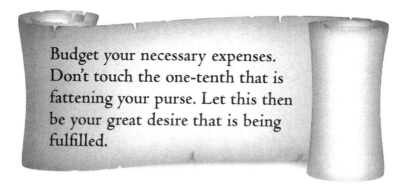

> Budget your necessary expenses.
> Don't touch the one-tenth that is
> fattening your purse. Let this then
> be your great desire that is being
> fulfilled.

"Keep working with your budget; keep adjusting it to help you. Make it your first assistant in defending your fattening purse."

Suddenly, one of the students, wearing an outfit of red and gold, got up and said, "I'm a free woman. I believe it's my right to enjoy the good things of life. From this moment, I rebel against the slavery of a budget supposedly determining just how much I can spend and for what. I feel it would take away too much pleasure from my life and make me feel like an ass from the olden days carrying a heavy burden."

Helen replied to her, "Who, my friend, would determine your budget?" "I'd make it for myself," responded the protester.

"In that case would that donkey's ass to budget her burden, would she include jewels and rugs and heavy loads of fancy furniture? No! She would include food and water, the necessities for the long desert trail.

"The purpose of a budget is to help you to fatten your purse. Understand, especially you younger women who are ever tempted to fritter away your money, I am not telling you to deprive your self of your whims and enjoyment of life. The budget is to assist you to have your necessities and as much as attainable, your other desires. It's to enable and *empower* you to realize your most cherished desires by defending them from your casual wishes. Like a bright light in a dark cave your budget shows up the leaks from your purse and assists you to stop them and control your spending on ever changing whims and temptations.

"In this way you will enjoy your indulgences. Continue also to always pay your self-first with that one tenth of your earnings, which you safely and diligently put away. Doing so will insure great comfort and security as you continue on life's often-precarious journey.

"This, then, is the second remedy for a lean purse. Budget your expenses so that you can have your golden money to pay for your necessities, to pay for your enjoyments and to indulge your worthwhile desires without spending more than nine- tenths of your earnings."

The Third Remedy—Make Your Moolah Multiply

CHAPTER FIVE

The Third Remedy—Make Your Moolah Multiply

"Be aware! Your lean purse is fattening. You have disciplined yourself to put one tenth, ten percent aside. You've controlled your expenditures to protect your growing treasure. Next, we will consider ways to put your treasure to work and to increase. Gold is a much more satisfying image than paper dollars. I prefer the word Gold instead of money. It is even my last name, as you know. Gold. So gold in a purse is gratifying to have and satisfies a miser but earns nothing. The gold we keep from our earnings is only the start girlfriends.

It's the earnings it makes that will build our fortunes." So Helen spoke on the third day to her class.

"How then can we put our gold to work? My first investment was unfortunate, for I lost all of it to the sexy bricklayer. I told you about this in our first talk. My first profitable investment was a loan I made to a man named Antonio, a brilliant jewelry designer. Once each year he bought large shipments of silver, lapis, rubies, sapphires, ancient Venetian glass beads and other stunning gems that he brought from across the ocean to use in his creations. Antonio lacked sufficient capital to pay the suppliers and he would borrow from those of us who had extra gold. He was an honorable man. He repaid his loan to me together with a substantial interest rate as he sold his jewelry.

"Each time I loaned to him I also loaned back the interest he had paid to me. Not only did my capital increase, but its earnings also increased. It was gratifying to have these sums return to my purse.

"I'm telling you my students, a woman's wealth is not in the moolah she carries in her purse; it's the income she builds, the golden stream that continually flows into her purse and keeps it always bulging."

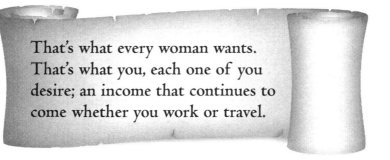

That's what every woman wants. That's what you, each one of you desire; an income that continues to come whether you work or travel.

"I've made a huge income. So huge that I'm called a very rich woman. My loans to Antonio were my first experiences in profitable investment. Gaining wisdom from this experience, I extended my loans and investments as my capital increased. From a few sources at first, from many sources later, a golden stream of wealth flowed into my purse available for whatever wise uses I chose.

"Consider, from my humble earnings I had created a heap of golden slaves, each working and earning more gold. As they worked for me, so their children also worked and their children's children until the income from their combined efforts was marvelous.

THE RICHEST WOMAN IN BABYLON AND MANHATTAN

"Gold increases quickly when you make a reasonable income as you will see from this parable from Babylon, the richest city in all of history, from which I've learned a great deal about how to achieve wealth here in Manhattan.

A farmer's wife, when her first daughter was born, took ten pieces of silver to a money lender and asked him to keep it on rental for her daughter until she became twenty years of age. This, the moneylender did, and agreed the rental, the interest, should be one- fourth or twenty-five percent of its value every four years. The farmer's wife asked, because this sum she had set aside as belonging to her daughter, that the interest be added to the principal.

"When the girl had reached the age of twenty years, the farmer's wife again went to the money lender to inquire about the silver. The moneylender explained that because this sum had been increased by compound interest, the original ten pieces of silver had now grown to thirty and one-half pieces.

"The farmer's wife was well pleased and because the daughter did not need the coins, she left them with the money lender. When the daughter became fifty years of age, the mother meantime having passed to the other world, the moneylender paid the daughter in settlement one hundred and sixty-seven pieces of silver!

"In fifty years the investment had multiplied itself with interest almost seventeen times.

"This, then, is the third remedy for a lean purse: to put each dollar to work so that it can reproduce itself, and help bring to you an income, a stream of wealth that flows constantly into your purse."

The Fourth Remedy—Guard Your Treasures From Loss

CHAPTER SIX

The Fourth Remedy—Guard Your Treasures From Loss

"Misfortune loves a shining mark. Gold in a woman's purse must be guarded with firmness, or it will be lost. We must first secure small amounts and learn to protect them before the Great Spirit and Goddess entrust us with larger amounts." So spoke Helen on the fourth day to her class.

"Every owner of gold, meaning money honey, is tempted by opportunities where it would seem that she could make large sums by investing in acceptable projects or ventures. Often friends and relatives are eagerly entering various investments and urge her to follow.

"The first sound principle of investment is security for your principal. Is it wise to be intrigued by larger earnings when your principal might be lost? I say no. The penalty of risk is probable loss. Study carefully, before parting with your treasure, every guarantee that it can be safely recovered. Don't be misled by your own romantic desires to make wealth quickly.

"Before you make a loan to any man or woman, assure yourself of their ability to repay *and* their reputation for doing so, and not mistakenly be making them a present of your hard-earned treasure."

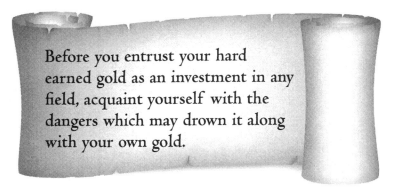

Before you entrust your hard earned gold as an investment in any field, acquaint yourself with the dangers which may drown it along with your own gold.

"My own first investment was a tragedy to me at the time. The guarded savings of a year I entrusted to that bricklayer, Marcus, who was traveling overseas and agreed to buy me the rare jewels of the island of Djerba. The plan was to sell them when he came back and we would divide the profits.

"The Tunisians were scoundrels and sold him bits of glass. My treasure was lost. Today, my training would immediately show me the foolishness of entrusting a bricklayer to buy jewels.

"Accordingly my dear ones, I advise you from the wisdom of my experiences: don't be too confident of your own wisdom in entrusting your treasured golden savings into the possible pitfalls of investments.

"Better by far to consult the wisdom of those experienced in handling money for profit. Investment advice is often free for the asking and may hold a value equal in gold to the sum you consider investing. The truth is that a personal financial expert can save you from regrettable loss. Do your homework and guard against banks that are corrupt and greedy lenders who feed you lies and deceit. We are living in times where finally there are "conscious" lenders and new styles of banking emerging to protect against the downfall of our local immoral and unethical Wall Street, now crumbling like the ancient Tower of Babel.

"This, then, is the fourth remedy for a lean purse, and of huge importance if it prevents your purse from being emptied once it's become fattened. Guard your treasure from loss by investing only where your principal is safe, where it can be reclaimed if needed, and where you won't fail to collect a fair interest rate. Consult with wise women and men. Get advice from people experienced in the profitable handling of money. Let their wisdom protect your treasure from unsafe investments."

The Fifth Remedy—Build Your Home Into A Profitable Investment

CHAPTER SEVEN

The Fifth Remedy—Build Your Home Into A Profitable Investment

"If a woman sets aside nine parts of her earnings to live on and enjoy life, and if she can turn any part of this nine parts into a profitable investment without detriment to her wellbeing, then all the much faster her treasures will grow." So spoke Helen to her class on the fifth day.

"All too many of our women of Manhattan raise their families in unseemly housing. They pay demanding landlords high rentals for apartments where their isn't a spot to raise the flowers that elate a woman's heart and their children have no place to play their games except in the unclean alleys.

"No woman's family can fully enjoy life unless they have a plot of land where children can play in the clean earth or a decent apartment with a balcony where the mother can raise not only flowers but good rich herbs and a few veggies to feed her family live, sacred, green nourishment.

"It brings joy to a woman's heart to eat the apples from her own trees and the grapes of her own vines. To own her own residence, a place she is proud to care for, puts confidence in her heart and greater effort behind all her activities. Consequently, I recommend that every woman own the roof that shelters her and hers.

"It's not beyond the ability of any well intentioned woman to own her home. Especially when lending rates are at an all time low. The real estate market has major periods when the market drops and prices are attainable, if only you have some money saved for a down payment. Consider also buying a house or condo outside of Manhattan or land to build on as an investment for the future.

"Also, my students know that lenders gladly consider the desires of women who seek homes and land for their families assuming you have not abused your credit by buying trifles or truffles," she laughed. "You can readily borrow to pay the contractor and the builder for such commendable reasons, or buy a condominium, if you can show a reasonable portion of the necessary sum which you've provided for this purpose.

"For this reason, you must keep your credit rating impeccable in order to qualify for a loan in the first place and to get it at the best possible rate of interest which can be the difference between you being able to afford the purchase or not."

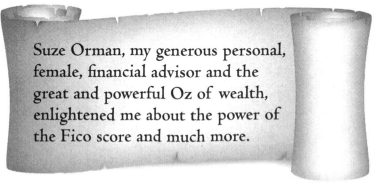

Suze Orman, my generous personal, female, financial advisor and the great and powerful Oz of wealth, enlightened me about the power of the Fico score and much more.

"Suze taught me this is a score used by banks, lenders, landlords and even employers to determine how good you are with your money. Find out today what your Fico score is.

"Then when the house is built or the condo purchased, you can pay the lender with the same regularity as you paid the landlord. Because each payment will reduce your debt to the lender, and in the years ahead you will pay off your loan. In this way you are also paying yourself.

"Then your heart will be thrilled because you will own in your own right a valuable property.

"Many blessings come to a woman who owns her own house. And if you buy wisely when the market is in your favor, it can greatly reduce your cost of living, increase your net worth, making available more of your earnings for pleasures and the gratification of your desires. This, then, is the fifth remedy for a lean purse: Own your own home and build it into a profitable investment."

The Sixth Remedy—Insure A Future Income

CHAPTER EIGHT

The Sixth Remedy—Insure A Future Income

"The life of every woman advances from her childhood to her old age. This is the path of life and no woman can deviate from it unless the Goddess calls her prematurely to leave the body for the world beyond. I'm telling you that it suits a woman to prepare for a suitable income in the days to come, when she's no longer a spring chicken, and to provide for her self or her family if she's no longer with them to take care of and support them. This lesson will instruct you in providing a full purse when time has made you less able to earn." So Helen addressed her class on the sixth day.

"The woman who, because of her understanding of the laws of wealth, and acquires a growing surplus should give thought to those future days. She should plan certain investments or provisions, which can endure safely for many years, and will be available when the time arrives.

"There are diverse ways by which a woman can provide safety and security for her future. She can provide a hiding place and bury a secret treasure. But, no matter how well she's hidden it, it may become loot for thieves. And what if her mind becomes feeble and suffers dementia and she forgets about her treasure entirely? Some of you are pooh-poohing, I see. Believe it or not, a lot of women still hide their money because they don't trust the banks or for other curious reasons. So I don't recommend this plan.

"A woman can buy houses or lands to provide for this purpose. If she buys wisely related to their usefulness and value in the future and holds on to the property then their value is permanent and their earnings or sale will provide well for her senior years.

"A woman can loan a small sum to ethical lenders and increase it at regular periods. The interest, which the lender gives, will add to its growth. Look for investments like CDs, Bonds and treasury bills that offer dividends. Suze Orman taught me to be sure the FDIC protects your lender. www.myfdicinsurance.gov

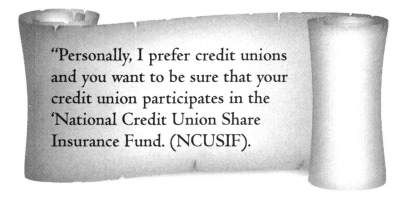

"Personally, I prefer credit unions and you want to be sure that your credit union participates in the 'National Credit Union Share Insurance Fund. (NCUSIF).

"Surely, when such a small contribution is made regularly, and produces profitable results, no woman can afford not to insure a treasure for her old age and the protection of her family, no matter how prosperous her business and her investments may be.

"The days ahead are unpredictable, the economy unstable and going through upheavals. Although there are many other, perhaps smarter savings plans that will give your family an inheritance, you may want to consider buying a term life insurance policy when you have started your family to assure leaving them a decent legacy to provide for times of uncertainty.

"I recommend to all women, that they, by wise and well thought out methods, do provide against a lean purse in their mature years. Ladies, a lean purse for a woman no longer able to earn or to a family without its head is a painful tragedy.

"This, then, is the sixth remedy for a lean purse. Provide in advance for the needs of your growing senior years and the protection of your family."

The Seventh Remedy—Increase Your Ability To Learn And Earn

CHAPTER NINE

The Seventh Remedy—Increase your ability to learn and earn

"Today I am going to speak to you, my devoted students, of one of the most vital remedies for a lean purse.

"And, I am not going to talk about money but I'm going to talk about YOU, the real you, not merely the women in stylish and maybe not so stylish outfits. I am speaking to your hearts and souls. My service here is to *inspire* and *instruct* you."

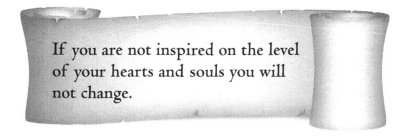

If you are not inspired on the level of your hearts and souls you will not change.

"I will talk to you of those things within the minds and lives of women that work for or against their success." This is how Helen addressed her class on the seventh day.

"Not long ago a young woman came to me to borrow money. When I questioned her about the cause of her necessity, she complained that her earnings were insufficient to pay her expenses. Then I explained to her, this being the case, she was a poor customer for the banks, as she possessed no surplus earning capacity to repay the loan.

"What you need, young woman,' I told her, 'is to earn more moolah darling. 'What do you do to increase your capacity to earn?'

"All that I can do' she replied. 'Six times within two months I approached my boss to ask for a raise, but without success. No woman can go more often than that."

"We may smile at her simplicity, yet she did possess one of the vital requirements to increase her earnings. Within her was a strong desire to earn more, a proper and commendable desire."

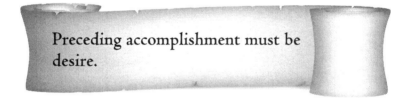

Preceding accomplishment must be desire.

"Your desires must be strong and definite. General desires are only weak longings. For a woman to wish to be rich is of little purpose. For a woman to desire one thousand dollars, that's a tangible desire, which she can press to fulfillment. After she has backed her desire for one thousand dollars with strength of purpose to secure it, next she can find similar ways to obtain ten thousand and then twenty thousand and later a hundred thousand dollars and, watch, she has become wealthy. In learning to secure her one definite small and achievable desire, she has trained herself to secure a larger one. This is the process by which wealth is accumulated: first in small sums, then in larger ones as a woman learns and becomes more capable." Again, desires must be strong and definite. They defeat their own purpose if they're too many, too confusing, or beyond a woman's training to accomplish.

"As a woman improves herself in her calling, her ability to earn also improves. In the days when I was a modest secretary typing documents every day, I observed that other employees did more than me and were paid more. That's when I became determined that I wouldn't be exceeded by any of them. And it didn't take long for me to discover the reason for their bigger success. With more interest in my work, more concentration on my job, more persistence in my effort, there were few women who could complete more documents in a day than me. With reasonable speed my increased skill was rewarded, and it wasn't necessary for me to go to my boss six times to ask for recognition."

> **The more wisdom we acquire, the more we may earn for our bodies and our souls.**

"That woman who seeks to learn more in her area of expertise will be richly rewarded. If she's an artist, she can learn the methods and the tools of those who are the most skillful in the same line. If she works as a lawyer or in the medical field, she can consult and exchange knowledge with others in her profession. If she operates her own business and is an entrepreneur, she can continually look for better products and services which can be bought at fair prices or create her own line of products and services.

"If she has an Internet web based business, she can generate a passive income with her own expertise, offering original products and services on her website that will fatten her purse while she sleeps. My own website line of downloadable products fills my purse 24-7. Think, what are you an expert in? You can create info products that offer wisdom and value to thousands of other women. Ladies I am planting seeds here. It is for you to water them and reap a satisfying harvest. Invest in learning with *conscious* women who can teach you the modern ways of Internet commerce. If this idea appeals to your senses, you can start this kind of venture on a part-time basis with a small start up cost.

"The affairs of woman always change and improve because savvy women always look for greater skill so they can better serve those whose patronage they depend on."

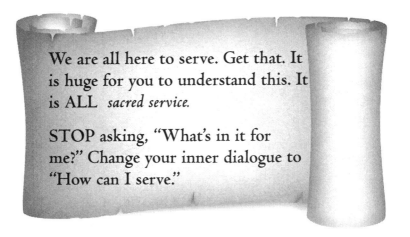

We are all here to serve. Get that. It is huge for you to understand this. It is ALL *sacred service.*

STOP asking, "What's in it for me?" Change your inner dialogue to "How can I serve."

"When I understood this wisdom taught to me by one of my greatest spiritual teachers, it changed my life. It will change yours too.

"I urge all women to be in the front rank of progress and not to stand still, in case they're left behind. Many things come to make a woman's life rich with transformational experiences. A woman must do the following things if she respects herself:

"She must pay her debts with all the promptness within her power, not buying anything that she is unable to pay for. She must take care of herself or her family so they can think and speak well of her. She must make a will, in case the Goddess calls her, in order that proper and honorable division of her property are seen to.

"She must have compassion upon those who are injured and smitten by misfortune and help them within reasonable limits. She must do acts of loving-kindness to those she cares for."

> She must learn to meditate, clean and clear her mind of stress, anxiety pain and suffering and become free from her addiction to thinking and endless desires.

"She must practice *sacred movement* with gentle yoga suitable for women and put *sacred nourishment* into her body with live, whole, fresh foods from the rainbow to enhance the wealth and health of her sacred body.

"She must drink freely from the *sacred breath* of life, learning how to breathe like the great yoginis. In this way, she will invite the Great Spirit indeed a

Holy Spirit that lives in the breath inside her breath. She must fill her cup with new prana and life force when her soul or her purse is lean.

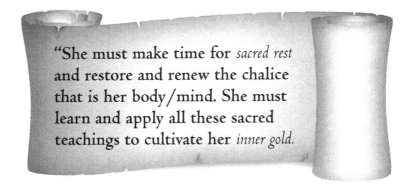

"She must make time for *sacred rest* and restore and renew the chalice that is her body/mind. She must learn and apply all these sacred teachings to cultivate her *inner gold.*

"Therefore, the seventh and last remedy for a lean purse is to cultivate your own powers, to study and become wiser, with masters of *financial* AND *spiritual* health.

"With all of this wisdom I have shared and learned from my beloved teachers with you, you too will gain confidence and peace in your self to achieve your carefully considered desires.

"These then are the seven remedies for a lean purse, which, out of my experience of a long and successful life, I urge all women who desire wealth. There is more golden wealth in America, my lovelies, than you could ever dream about. There's abundance for all to fill your shabby purses and illuminate your weary souls. Financial and spiritual health is abundant for those who know the seven timeless remedies and how to get it, keep it and make it grow.

"Now go out into your life and **TAKE ACTION, practice these truths** that you can prosper and grow wealthy in body, mind and spirit which is your right.

"Go and also **share and teach these truths** so that every honorable women can share liberally in the ample wealth of our beloved city and nation."

On that very day Ambha, the nurse, healer and yoga teacher and Melanie the caterer, artist and raw food chef were transformed and transcended. It was the beginning of bountiful success for both of them.

In good time they filled their purses and illuminated their hearts and souls. They became respected leaders, change agents and women of power and influence in their respective fields. They generously shared this timeless wisdom with all who had eyes to see and ears to hear.

Let those who have eyes to see, *see.*
Let those who have ears to hear, *hear.*

The Richest Woman in Babylon

CHAPTER TEN

The Richest Woman in Babylon

"*If a woman be lucky, there is no foretelling the possible extent of her good fortune. Pitch her into the Hudson River and like as not she will swim out with a pearl in her hand.*" —Babylonian and Manhattan proverb.

The desire to be lucky is universal. It was just as strong in the breasts of women four thousand years ago in ancient Babylon as it is in the hearts of women today. We all hope to be favored by the whimsical Goddess of Good Luck.

Is there some way we can meet her and attract, not only her favorable attention, but also her generous favors? Is there a way to attract good luck? That is what the women of ancient Babylon wished to know. It is exactly what they decided to find out.

Babylonians had no schools or colleges. Nevertheless they had a center of learning and a very practical one it was. Among the towered buildings in Babylon was one that ranked in importance with the Palace of the King, the Hanging Gardens and the temples of the Gods.

In that distant past, they had no schools or colleges. Nevertheless they had a center of learning and a very practical one it was. Among the towered buildings in Babylon was one that ranked in importance with the Palace of the King, the Hanging Gardens and the temples of the Gods. You will find scant mention of it in the history books, more likely no mention at all, yet it exerted a powerful influence upon the thought of that time.

This building was the Temple of Learning where the wisdom of the past was expounded by voluntary teachers and where subjects of popular interest were discussed in open forums. Within its walls all women met as equals. There was a separate chamber for the wise women and the female students who congregated there, which was parted from the chambers of the men who naturally also gathered there. The humblest of slaves could dispute with impunity the opinions of a princess of the royal house.

Among the many who frequented the Temple of Learning, was **a beautiful, wise rich woman named Helena, called the richest woman in Babylon.**

She had her own special hall where almost any evening a large group of women, some old, some very young, but mostly middle-aged, gathered to discuss and argue interesting subjects. These women were free to bring their children, and could settle in without worry for their little ones. Suppose we listen in to see whether they knew how to attract good luck.

The sun had just set like a great red ball of fire shining through the haze of desert dust when Helena strolled regally to her accustomed platform. Already full four score women were awaiting her arrival, reclining on their small rugs spread upon the floor. More were still arriving.

"What shall we discuss this night?" Helena inquired.

After a brief hesitation, a petite silk cloth weaver addressed her, arising as was the custom. "I have a subject I would like to hear discussed yet hesitate to offer lest it seem ridiculous to you, Helena, and my good friends here."

Upon being urged to offer it, both by Helena and by calls from the others, she continued: "This day I have been lucky, for I have found a purse in which there are pieces of gold. To continue to be lucky is my great desire. Feeling that all women share with me this desire, I do suggest we debate how to attract good luck that we may discover ways it can be enticed by all."

"A most interesting subject has been offered, Helena commented, "one most worthy of our discussion. To some women, good luck bespeaks but a chance happening that, like an accident, may befall one without purpose or reason. Others do believe that the instigator of all good fortune is our most bounteous goddess, Shakti, ever anxious to reward with generous gifts those who please her. Speak up, my friends, what say you, shall we seek to find if there be means by which good luck may be enticed to visit each and all of us?"

"Yea! Yea! And much of it!" responded the growing group of eager listeners.

Thereupon Helena continued, "To start our discussion, let us first hear from those among us who have enjoyed experiences similar to that of the cloth weaver in finding or receiving, without effort upon their part, valuable treasures or jewels."

There was a pause in which all looked about expecting someone to reply but no one did.

""What, no one?" Helena said, "then rare indeed must be this kind of good luck. Who now will offer a suggestion as to where we shall continue our search?"

"That I will do," spoke a well-robed middle-aged woman, arising. "When a woman speaketh of luck is it not natural that her thoughts turn to the gaining tables? It is not only our men who enjoy the sport of betting in these modern days in Babylon. Is it not there at these tables of luck, we find many women courting the favor of the goddess in hope she will bless them with rich winnings?"

As she resumed her seat a voice called, "Do not stop! Continue thy story! Tell us, didst thou find favor with the goddess at the gaming tables? Did she turn the cubes with red side up so thou filled thy purse at the dealer's expense or did she permit the blue sides to come up so the dealer raked in thy hard- earned pieces of silver?"

The woman joined the good-natured laughter, and then replied, "I am not opposed to admitting she seemed not to know I was even there, but how about the rest of you? Have you found her waiting about such places to roll the cubes, in your favor? We are eager to hear as well as to learn."

"A wise start," broke in Helena. "We meet here to consider all sides of each question. To ignore the gaming table of chance would be to overlook an instinct common to most women, the love of taking a chance with a small amount of silver in the hope of winning much gold."

"That doth remind me of the races but yesterday, where many of our men in Babylon court the Goddess" called out another listener. "If the goddess frequents the gaming tables, certainly she dost not overlook the races where the gilded chariots and the foaming horses offer far more excitement. Tell us honestly, Helena, didst she whisper to you to place your bet upon those grey horses from Nineveh yesterday? I was standing just behind thee with my husband and could scarce believe my ears when I heard thee place thy bet upon the greys. Thou knowest as well as any of us that no team in all Assyria can beat our beloved bays in a fair race.

"Didst the goddess whisper in thy ear to bet upon the greys because at the last turn the inside black would stumble and so interfere with our bays that the greys would win the race and score an unearned victory?"

Helena smiled indulgently at the banter. "What reason have we to feel the good goddess would take that much interest in any woman's bet upon a horse race? To me she is a goddess of love and dignity whose pleasure it is to aid those who are in need and to reward those who are deserving. I look to find her, not at the gaming tables or the races where men lose more gold than they win but in other places where the doings of women are more worthwhile and more worthy of reward.

"In tilling the soil of your gardens, in the crafting and design of sundry items, in cooking, in the study of medicinal herbs, teaching, nursing the sick and wounded, in honest trading, in all of woman's occupations, there is opportunity to make a profit upon her efforts and her transactions. Perhaps not all the time will she be rewarded because sometimes her judgment may be faulty and other times the winds and the weather may defeat her efforts. Yet, if she persists, she may usually expect to realize her profit. This is so because the chances of profit are always in her favor.

"But, when a woman playeth the games, the situation is reversed for the chances of profit are always against her and always in favor of the game keeper. The game is so arranged that it will always favor the keeper. It is the business of men, business at which a man plans to make a liberal profit for himself from the coins bet by the players. Few players realize how certain are the gamekeeper's profits and how uncertain are their own chances to win.

"For example, let us consider wagers placed upon the cube. Each time it is cast we bet which side will be uppermost. If it be the red side the game master pays to us four times our bet. But if any other of the five sides comes uppermost, we lose our bet. Thus the figures show that for each cast we have five chances to lose, but because the red pays four for one, we have four chances to win. In a night's play the game master can expect to keep for his profit one-fifth of all the coins wagered. Can a woman or a man expect to win more than occasionally against odds so arranged that she should lose one-fifth of all her bets?"

"Yet some do win large sums at times," volunteered one of the listeners.

"Quite so, they do," Helena continued. "Realizing this, the question comes to me whether money secured in such ways brings permanent value to those who are thus lucky. Among my acquaintances are many of the successful men of Babylon, yet among them I am unable to name a single one who started his success from such a source.

"You who are gathered here tonight know many more of our substantial citizens. To me it would be of much interest to learn how many of our successful citizens can credit the gaming tables with their start to success. Suppose each of you tell of those you know. What say you?"

After a prolonged silence, a wag ventured, 'Wouldst thy inquiry include the game keepers?" "If you think of no one else," Helena responded.

"If not one of you can think of anyone else, then how about yourselves? Are there any consistent winners with us who hesitate to advise such a source for their incomes?"

Her challenge was answered by a series of groans from the rear taken up and spread amid much laughter.

"It would seem we are not seeking good luck in such places as the goddess frequents," she continued. "Therefore let us explore other fields. We have not found it in picking up lost wallets.

Neither have we found it haunting the gaming tables. As to the races, I must confess to have lost far more coins there than I have ever won.

"Now, suppose we consider our trades and businesses. Is it not natural if we conclude a profitable transaction to consider it not good luck but a just reward for our efforts? I am inclined to think we may be overlooking the gifts of the goddess. Perhaps she really does assist us when we do not appreciate her generosity. Who can suggest further discussion?"

Thereupon an elderly merchant arose, smoothing her genteel white robe. "With thy permission, most honorable Helena and my friends, I offer a suggestion. If, as you have said, we take credit to our own industry and ability for our business success, why not consider the successes we almost enjoyed but which escaped us, happenings which would have been most profitable. They would have been rare examples of good luck if they had actually happened. Because they were not brought to fulfillment we cannot consider them as our just rewards. Surely many women here have such experiences to relate."

"Here is a wise approach," Helena approved. "Who among you have had good luck within your grasp only to see it escape?"

Many hands were raised, among them that of the merchant. Helena motioned to her to speak.

"As you suggested this approach, we should like to hear first from you."

"I will gladly relate a tale," she resumed, "that doth illustrate how closely unto a woman good luck may approach and how blindly she may permit it to escape, much to her loss and later regret.

"Many years ago when I was a young woman, just married and well-started to earning, my father did come one day and urge most strongly that I and my husband enter in an investment. The son of one of his good friends had taken notice of a barren tract of land not far beyond the outer walls of our city. It lay high above the canal where no water could reach it.

"The son of my father's friend devised a plan to purchase this land, build three large water wheels that could be operated by oxen and thereby raise the life-giving waters to the fertile soil. This accomplished, he planned to divide into small tracts and sell to the residents of the city for medicinal herb patches.

"The son of my father's friend did not possess sufficient gold to complete such an undertaking. Like my husband, he was a young man earning a fair sum. His father, like mine, was a man of large family and small means. He, therefore, decided to interest a group of men and women to enter the enterprise with him. The group was to comprise twelve, each of whom must be a money earner and agree to pay one-tenth of his or her earnings into the enterprise until the land was made ready for sale. All would then share justly in the profits in proportion to their investment."

'My daughter and new son-in law,' bespoke my father, 'art now in thy young womanhood and manhood. It is my deep desire that thee begin the building of a valuable estate for yourselves that thee mayest become respected in our city. I desire to see thee profit from a knowledge of the thoughtless mistakes of thy father."

"This do we most ardently desire, my father," I replied.

"Then, this do I advise. Do what I should have done at thy age. From thy earnings keep out one-tenth to put into favorable investments. With this one- tenth of thy earnings and what it will also earn, thou canst, before thou art my age, accumulate for thyself a valuable estate.

"Thy words are words of wisdom, my father. Greatly do we desire riches. Yet there are many uses to which our earnings are called. Therefore, do I hesitate to do as thou dost advise. We are young. There is plenty of time."

"So I thought at thy age, yet behold, many years have passed and I have not yet made the beginning."

"We live in a different age, my father. We shall avoid thy mistakes."

"Opportunity stands before thee, my children. It is offering a chance that may lead to wealth. I beg of thee, do not delay. Go upon the morrow to the son of my friend and bargain with him to pay ten percent of thy earnings into this investment. Go promptly upon the morrow. Opportunity waits for no man. Today it is here; soon it is gone. Therefore, delay not!"

"In spite of the advice of my father, my husband and I did hesitate. There were beautiful new robes just brought by the tradesmen from the East, robes of such richness and beauty and we felt we must each possess one. Should I agree to pay one-tenth of my earnings into the enterprise, we must deprive ourselves of these and other pleasures we dearly desired. I delayed making a decision until it was too late, much to my subsequent regret. The enterprise did prove to be more profitable than any man had prophesied. This is my tale, showing how I did permit good luck to escape."

"In this tale we see how good luck waits to come to that woman who accepts opportunity," commented a swarthy woman of the desert. "To the building of an estate there must always be the beginning. That start may be a few pieces of gold or silver which a woman diverts from her earnings to her first investment. I, myself, am the owner of many herds. The start of my herds I did begin when I was a mere girl working along side of boys as a shepherd-ess, and did purchase with one piece of silver a young calf. This, being the beginning of my wealth, was of great importance to me.

"To take her first start to building an estate is as good luck as can come to any woman. With all women, that first step, which changes them from women who earn from their own labor to women who draw dividends from the earnings of their gold, is important. Some, fortunately, take it when young and thereby outstrip in financial success those who do take it later or those unfortunate women, like the father of this merchant, who never take it.

"Had our friend, the merchant, taken this step in her early womanhood when this opportunity came to her, this day she would be blessed with much more of this world's goods. Should the good luck of our friend, the cloth weaver, cause her to take such a step at this time, it will indeed be but the beginning of much greater good fortune."

"Thank you! I like to speak, also." A stranger from another country arose. "I am a Syrian. Not so well do I speak your tongue. I wish to call this friend, the merchant woman, a name. Maybe you think it not polite, this name. Yet I wish to call her that. But, alas, I not know your word for it. If I do call it in Syrian, you will not understand. Therefore, please some good gentlewomen, tell me that right name you call woman who puts off doing those things that mighty good for her."

"Procrastinator," called a voice.

"That's her," shouted the Syrian, waving her hands excitedly, "she accepts not opportunity when she comes. She waits. She says I have much business right now. Bye and bye I talk to you. Opportunity, she will not wait for such slow sister. She thinks if a woman desires to be lucky she will step quick. Any woman not step quick when opportunity comes, she big procrastinator like our friend, this merchant."

The merchant arose and bowed good-naturedly in response to the laughter. "My admiration to thee, stranger within our gates, who hesitates not to speak the truth."

"And now let us hear another tale of opportunity. Who has for us another experience?" demanded Helena.

"I have," responded a red-robed woman of middle age. "My family be buyers of animals, mostly camels and horses. Sometimes I do also buy the sheep and goats when my husband is other wise occupied. The tale I am about to relate will tell truthfully how opportunity came one night when I did least expect it. Perhaps for this reason I did let it escape. Of this you shall be the judge.

"Returning to the city one evening after a disheartening ten- days' journey in search of camels, I was much angered to find the gates of the city closed and locked. While my slaves spread our tent for the night, which we looked to spend with little food and no I water, I was approached by an elderly farmer who, like ourselves, found himself locked outside.

"'Honored wise woman,' he addressed me, 'from thy appearance, I do judge thee to be a buyer. If this be so, much would I like to sell to thee as the most excellent flock of sheep just driven up. Alas, my good wife lies very sick with the fever. I must return with all haste. Buy thou my sheep that I and my slaves may mount our camels and travel back without delay."

"So dark it was that I could not see his flock, but from the bleating I did know it must be large.

"Having wasted ten days searching for camels I could not find, I was glad to bargain with him. In his anxiety, he did set a most reasonable price. I accepted, well knowing my slaves could drive the flock through the city gates in the morning and sell at a substantial profit.

'The bargain concluded, I called my slaves to bring torches that we might count the flock which the farmer declared to contain nine hundred. I shall not burden you, my friends, with a description of our difficulty in attempting to count so many thirsty, restless, milling sheep. It proved to be an impossible task. Therefore, I bluntly informed the farmer I would count them at daylight and pay him then.

"Please, most honorable lady,' he pleaded, 'pay me but two-thirds of the price tonight that I may be on my way. I will leave my most intelligent and educated slave to assist to make the count in the morning. He is trustworthy and to him thou canst pay the balance.

"But I was stubborn and refused to make payment that night for my husband had tutored me to be sure to get an accurate count before payment to any farmers. Next morning, before I awoke, the city gates opened and four buyers rushed out in search of flocks. They were most eager and willing to pay high prices because the city was threatened with siege, and food was not plentiful. Nearly three times the price at which he had offered the flock to me did the old farmer receive for it. Thus was rare good luck allowed to escape," and she sighed deeply.

"Here is a tale most unusual," commented Helena. "What wisdom doth it suggest?"

"The wisdom of making a payment immediately when we are convinced our bargain is wise," suggested a venerable wife of a saddle maker. "If the bargain be good, then dost thou need protection against thy own weaknesses as much as against any other woman or man. We mortals are changeable. Alas, I must say more apt to change our minds when right than wrong. Wrong, we are stubborn indeed. Right, we are prone to vacillate and let opportunity escape. My first judgment is my best. Yet always have I found it difficult to compel myself to proceed with a good bargain when made at the market. Therefore, as a protection against my own weaknesses, I do make a prompt deposit thereon. This doth save me from later regrets for the good luck that should have been mine."

"Thank you! Again I like to speak." The Syrian woman was upon her feet once more. "These tales much alike. Each time opportunity fly away for same reason. Each time she come to procrastinator, bringing good plan. Each time they hesitate, not say, right now best time, I do it quick. How can women succeed that way?"

"Wise are thy words, my friend," responded the buyer. "Good luck fled from procrastination in both these tales. Yet, this is not unusual. The spirit of procrastination is within all women and men. We desire riches; yet, how often when opportunity doth appear before us, that spirit of procrastination from within doth urge various delays in our acceptance.

"In listening to it we do become our own worst enemies. In my younger days I did not know it by this long word our friend from Syria doth enjoy. I did think at first it was my own poor judgment that did cause me loss of many profitable trades. Later, I did credit it to my stubborn disposition. At last, I did recognize it for what it was—a habit of needless delaying where action was required, action prompt and decisive. How I did hate it when its true character stood revealed. With the bitterness of a wild ass hitched to a chariot, I did break loose from this enemy to my success."

"Thank you! I like ask question from Mrs. Merchant." The Syrian was speaking.

"You wear fine robes, not like those of poor woman. You speak like successful woman. Tell us, do you listen now when procrastination whispers in your ear?"

"Like our friend the buyer, I also had to recognize and conquer procrastination," responded the merchant. "To me, it proved to be an enemy, ever watching and waiting to thwart my accomplishments.

"The tale I did relate is but one of many similar instances I could tell to show how it drove away my opportunities. Tis not difficult to conquer, once understood. No woman willingly permits the thief to rob her bins of grain. Nor does any woman willingly permit an enemy to drive away her customers and rob her of her profits. When once I did recognize that such acts as these my enemy was committing, with determination I conquered it. So must every woman master her own spirit of procrastination before she can expect to share in the rich treasures of Babylon."

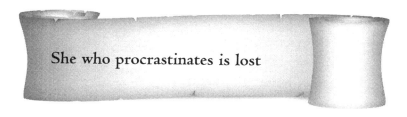

She who procrastinates is lost

"Because thou art the richest woman in Babylon, many do proclaim thee to be the luckiest. Dost thou agree with me that no woman can arrive at a full measure of success until she hath completely crushed the spirit of procrastination within her?"

"It is even as thou sayest," Helena admitted. "During my long life I have watched generation following generation, marching forward along those avenues of trade, science and learning that lead to success in life.

"Opportunities came to all these citizens. Some grasped theirs and moved steadily to the gratification of their deepest desires, but the majority hesitated, faltered and fell behind."

Helena turned to the cloth weaver. "Thou didst suggest that we debate good luck. Let us hear what thou now thinkest upon the subject."

"I do see good luck in a different light. I had thought of it as something most desirable that might happen to a woman without effort upon her part. Now, I do realize such happenings are not the sort of thing one may attract to herself. From our discussion have I learned that to attract good luck to oneself, it is necessary to take advantage of opportunities, therefore, in the future, I shall endeavor to make the best of such opportunities as do come to me."

"Thou hast well grasped the truths brought forth in our discussion," Helena replied. "Good luck, we do find, often follows opportunity but seldom comes otherwise. Our merchant friend would have found great good luck had she accepted the opportunity the good goddess did present to her. Our friend the buyer, likewise, would have enjoyed good luck had she completed the purchase of the flock and sold at such a handsome profit.

"We did pursue this discussion to find a means by which good luck could be enticed to us. I feel that we have found the way. Both the tales did illustrate how good luck follows opportunity.

"Herein lies a truth that many similar tales of good luck, won or lost, could not change.

"The truth is this: Good luck can be enticed by accepting opportunity.

"Those eager to grasp opportunities for their betterment do attract the interest of the good goddess. She is ever anxious to aid those who please her. "Women of action please her best. Action will lead thee forward to the successes you desire and you will be favored by the goddess of good luck."

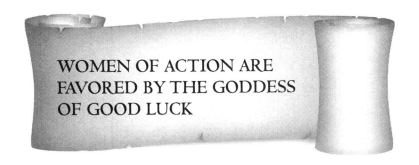

WOMEN OF ACTION ARE
FAVORED BY THE GODDESS
OF GOOD LUCK

TAKE ACTION

With

AGELESS WISDOM from

THE RICHEST WOMAN IN BABYLON

+

SEVEN *TIMELESS* REMEDIES from

THE RICHEST WOMAN IN MANHATTAN

&

BEGIN TO FATTEN YOUR PURSE

+

ILLUMINATE YOUR SOUL

TODAY

RESOURCES

This is a list of all the peeps I have wisely invested in who have helped me to fatten my purse + illuminate my soul.

Aham: Happiness Now with the Practice of Self-Inquiry www.aham.com

Arielle Ford: Soul Mate Secrets + Secrets to Financial Success
www.arielleford.com

Brendon Burchard: The Millionaire Messenger www.brendonburchard.com

Renae Bechthold: Metro Marketing and Media www.metromm.com

JW Dicks and Nick Nanton, Celebrity Branding:
www.CelebrityBrandingAgency.com

Danielle LaPorte: Light Your Fire Soul Entrepreneur
www.whitehottruth.com

Alexandra Franzen: Wordsmith + Creator Leading to Profits
www.alexandrafranzen.com

Kady Laloo: Nurse Turned Eccentric Web Designer
www.eccentrichusky.com

Mynde Mayfield: Custom Design + Life & Business Coaching
www.myndemayfield.com

Christine Kloser: Transformational Authors
www.transformationalauthors.com

Kripalu Yoga Center: Leader in Health Programs www.kripalu.org

Simple Banking: Rachel Giuliani, A New Style of Conscious Banking
www.simple.com

Stephanie Gunning: Get a Book Deal www.stephaniegunning.com

Susan Harrow: Sell Yourself Without Selling Your Soul
www.prsecrets.com

Suzie Orman: Financial Guru www.suzeorman.com

Patricia Raskin's: Positive Living www.raskinresources.com

Elaine Wilkes: Natural Solutions Expert, Writing Coach
www.elainewilkes.com

ACKNOWLEDGEMENTS

Infinite gratitude to my mother Anna and father Joseph, an entrepreneur, who taught me to invest in land and good opportunities, my son Julian Proulx, my hero Gaetan Proulx, brother Joe Tersigni, niece Rachelle Tersigni, Zia Emilia, my first spiritual teacher, who inspired my love for the saints and introduced me to Dante's Divine Comedy. Hugo and Anne Maier, A. Ramana, Deepak Chopra MD, David Simon MD, Arielle Ford, Lindsay Dicks, J.W. Dicks, Nick Nanton, Brendon Burchard, Renae Bechthold, Miriam Gotlib, Ellen Levine, Theo Halmay, Kady Laloo R.N., Vandita Kate Marchesiello, Alcida Boissoneault, Kate Loving Shenk R.N., Susan Ketchin, Penny and Mark Hooper, Barb Stanislawski, Anna Morrison R.N., Dr. Lisa Vitesse, Robert Bregman, Thomas Ryan CPS, Nell Thompson, Linda McGregor, Jeri McConkey, Judith Mintz, Myrna Santos R.N., Elaine Wilkes author-coach, Shane Willis artistic wizard, Steven Ehrlick scrutinizing editor, Patricia Raskin the queen of positive radio, Suze Orman the Goddess of finance, Maria Galati Smith my wise media consultant, Stephanie Gunning who unleashed my writing muse, Susan Harrow the Goddess of PR, to countless savvy saints and sinners who have been my teachers, and to the manliest man I know, Manly Mason, you are my anchor.

Finally to Melanie Dunkelman, chef, artist and caterer extraordinaire and Helen Goldstein, real estate maven, creatrix, and the doyenne of Canadian yoga, who were the inspiration for the leading characters in this book, I adore you both forever and a day.

ABOUT THE AUTHOR

Annette Tersigni R.N., known as the Yoga Nurse, is a former Hollywood actor and cover girl turned nurse — healer and 'health care rebel *with* a cause.' A practical mystic, author, speaker, teacher, and seminar leader, she is the founder of Yoga Nursing: a new lifestyle brand and trend in health care, nursing and yoga. A successful entrepreneur, Annette is 'expanding consciousness in health care' and is saving and transforming lives physically, financially and spiritually. A frequent guest of the media, she has appeared on ABC, NBC, CBS and FOX news affiliates. Giving Sacred Service with her Sacred Remedy to relieve stress, anxiety, pain and suffering, Annette is beloved by thousands of students and patients who have realized life changing benefits through her wisdom, compassion and caring.

Yoga Nurse

Contact Annette for interviews or speaking engagements at
www.yoganurse.com or annette@yoganurse.com

Other books by this author:

Yoga Nursing: the Heart of Caring: A training guide for nurses

Health Care Rebel With A Cause: A new Rx + sacred remedy to relieve stress, anxiety, pain and suffering

"The Truth Is Always In Fashion."

Annette Tersigni R.N., The Yoga Nurse

www.yoganurse.com

NOTES

NOTES

NOTES

NOTES

NOTES

Made in the USA
Lexington, KY
08 February 2012